FULLY HUMAN

A PREPONDERANCE OF APHORISMS TO PONDER

DAVID L. LAING

Copyright © 2024 by David L. Laing

Book design and editing by Marilyn E. Dillon

Cover and editing by Adam Douglas Heyes

All rights reserved.

No part of this book may be reproduced in any form or by any electronic or mechanical means, including information storage and retrieval systems, without written permission from the author, except for the use of brief quotations in a book review.

Published in the United States of America

Cosmic Art Center

62 Cedar St., Apt. 601

Seattle, Washington 98121

Paperback ISBN 978-1-960089-14-4

CONTENTS

Definition   5

Foreword   7

Aphorisms   11

About the Author   89

Purchasing Artwork and Connecting   90

Also by David L. Laing   91

APHORISM

a concise statement of a principle;

a terse formulation of a truth or sentiment

—Merriam-Webster Dictionary

FOREWORD

Fully Human is the fourth volume of David L. Laing's series of aphorism books. The series began with aphorisms 1 to 750 in *Not Yet Human*, followed by aphorisms 751 to 1500 in *Almost Human,* and aphorisms 1501 to 2250 in *Just Human*. This book presents another 750 pithy sayings. *Beyond Human* is forthcoming, with another 750 aphorisms, and several more aphorism books are in the works!

How can anyone write so many? You may well wonder, and the only answer is David L. Laing's boundless reservoirs of creativity. He has more ideas than he can get expressed, whether in words or images. In fact, he keeps a list of ideas he hopes to bring into being. It resides on a roll of paper that, at last report, was more than 40 feet long.

So, please keep reading. Take your time with David Laing's writings. They're filled with wisdom and word-play. They may be metaphorical or humorous, earthy or ethereal. The next aphorism may be the insight that speaks to you directly. It will probably be a surprise, as the only organization here is randomness.

If you go with his flow, David Laing will keep you pondering, meditating, admiring his unique drawings, and maybe coloring some of them. There are lots of books now (see page 91), and more on the way.

Until next time…

FULLY HUMAN

APHORISMS

—2251—

Language is wise seen through a guise.

—2252—

Evolving is love the solving.

—2253—

Cosmos within—inner expands outer.

—2254—

Pathfinder is truth binder.

—2255—

There is know meaning.

—2256—

Tail the comet's trail.

—2257—

It is no ruse when literature and philosophy fuse.

—2258—

Too eager to share advice is a vice.

—2259—

Wealth of words does not make an idea rich.

—2260—

Hide to reveal inside.

—2261—

Gory when glory is the whole story.

—2262—

Strike out on your own—
dig out, no return to the dugout.

—2263—

Psychology is never bankrupt—
credit from the "Imagination Bank."

—2264—

Understand gods becoming one.

—2265—

Surpass impasse.

—2266—

Tell intelligence by sense.

—2267—

Elevation—elation—revelation.

—2268—

Simply becoming undivided is not simple.

—2269—

Certainty is uncertainty for certain.

—2270—

Camel hump is over its hump.

—2271—

Transform prevailing norm with transcendent form.

—2272—

Frame discipline with its own name.

—2273—

Aloof transcends its roof.

—2274—

The hole in whole is whole.

—2275—

Pure literature is its own nature.

—2276—

We are the pen—our blood the ink.

—2277—

Earth has its own breath.

—2278—

Work free-standing has legs of understanding.

—2279—

Magic is imagination—the will to distill.

—2280—

A stoic is planted poetic.

—2281—

Bell-shaped flowers continue ringing
long after the temple bell has ended singing.

—2282—

Image of rare knowledge is a sage.

—2283—

Shape of a tree is a giant leaf—
hologram in relief.

—2284—

The perfect match strikes the match.

—2285—

Knowledge through intuition is certain and uncertain.

—2286—

Growing up is not growing up.

—2287—

The weight of the world and word are often not in balance.

—2288—
Accentuate the bounding line—
square or round it is fine.

—2289—
Nobility is ability plus vulnerability.

—2290—
Unreel—feel the real.

—2291—
Choice: fall or fly.

—2292—
Picture improvisation as future civilization.

—2293—
What rode is in code.

—2294—
Metaphor is metamorphosis.

—2295—
A depressed mountain is a valley.

—2296—
Self-esteem is steam driven to stay on track.

—2297—
Difference between palace and hovel
is one is dug with a shovel.

—2298—

We are subjects of subjective and objects of objective.

—2299—

Words contain the secret and the secret contains words.

—2300—

Before the fall the ALL had no wall.

—2301—

Something is a thing for some.

—2302—

Add a sun and you have a system.

—2303—

Speak to experience the "peak."

—2304—

Existentialism is survival outfit for the misfit.

—2305—

Define a line—decline to stay in line.

—2306—

Words hope to be microscope and telescope.

—2307—

Creative minority is active majority.

—2308—

Struggle in vain between the left and the right brain.

—2309—

Tumultuous tango takes two words to tangle.

—2310—

Occupy the mind in planetary revolution.

—2311—

Genius thrives in uncertainty, chaos and pandemonium.

—2312—

Mind empty filled with mankind.

—2313—

Words cross at the crossroads.

—2314—

Experience the peak—

mountain is not weak.

—2315—

The world is a patchwork quilt of wrinkles of guilt.

—2316—

Cosmic man in no fixed place—

occupies anywhere in space.

—2317—

What is outside was first inside and not the contrary.

—2318—
Mind-at-Large with soul in charge.

—2319—
Earth opposes dearth.

—2320—
Awash in cosmic consciousness—
no motivation to give the dishes a wash.

—2321—
God is complete self-knowledge.

—2322—
Write the story of the age is pilgrimage.

—2323—
Turn the ineffable into fable—turntable.

—2324—
Narrowing consciousness is boredom,
widening it a kingdom.

—2325—
Female waterfall rose after she fell.

—2326—
Literal is not literary—a building is not a library.

—2327—
Ponder the universe to traverse in wonder.

—2328—

The enemy of mysticism is academicism.

—2329—

Thank paper that is blank.

—2330—

Ink helps to think—a mind well drawn from an ink well.

—2331—

Innocence is the ultimate sophistication.

—2332—

Knowledge is limited—creativity is not.

—2333—

Demiurge fashioned the world on a creative urge.

—2334—

The matter of mind is the mind of matter.

—2335—

Intolerance is not part of the dance.

—2336—

Don't miss undiluted bliss.

—2337—

Explain the epic battle waged between the old and new brain.

—2338—
Eternal feminine is a fine line.

—2339—
Mystical spiral goes viral.

—2340—
We live in an age of mirage.

—2341—
What closes the mind—opens it.

—2342—
Jesus is exegesis.

—2343—
Boxed in or beyond the box.

—2344—
The One needs everybody.

—2345—
Play the part of the planet.

—2346—
Luminous to literary—lighthouse to library.

—2347—
Straddle the "Imagination horse" staying in the saddle.

—2348—

Feminine is discipline.

—2349—

Need a moving body to embody a body of knowledge.

—2350—

Treasure maps pleasure.

—2351—

Logic and reason can dehydrate a season.

—2352—

Overcome pain to develop the brain.

—2353—

Caravel is the head marvel.

—2354—

Crime opposes time.

—2355—

Body and spirit share a mutual muse.

—2356—

A sage can gauge the age of language.

—2357—

The teacher is the student.

—2358—

Nature is stature.

—2359—

Sexual is circular.

—2360—

Figurative precedes the literal.

—2361—

Seer of old has a chest full of stories untold.

—2362—

Natural opium is a personal compendium.

—2363—

Difference between plus and minus is a line-up.

—2364—

Vision first begun with orison to the sun.

—2365—

Incense makes good sense in scent sense.

—2366—

John Stuart Mill tried to put out fires of depression with buckets of happiness.

—2367—

Aristotle's categories are not stories.

—2368—

Plato stayed in shape using forms to wrestle with ideas.

—2369—

God is the guide dog.

—2370—

Power is play—play is power.

—2371—

Master mystery is history.

—2372—

Poetry affirms—prose confirms.

—2373—

Imagination is a shape-shifting nation.

—2374—

A haiku is not about "u."

—2375—

Vex what comes next to make a text complex.

—2376—

Manic tries to overcome panic.

—2377—

Boots search for metaphysical roots.

—2378—

Nothing is not "no-thing" but everything.

—2379—

Life slice is filled with virtue and vice.

—2380—

Current events have electricity running through their vents.

—2381—

The active difference between the sultan and subject is subjective.

—2382—

In its day, the Silk Road was an earthly milky way.

—2383—

Enchanted takes nothing for granted.

—2384—

Know the world before it can know you.

—2385—

Not ill, the human bean sprouts at will.

—2386—

Dismembered—but remembered.

—2387—

Light electricity for the invisible city.

—2388—

Old texts—new contexts.

—2389—

As pencil and eraser—God's way to giveth and taketh away.

—2390—

The pen flows with thought till it runs dry in drought.

—2391—

Forsaken—the world cannot awaken nor be taken.

—2392—

Hopeless and helpless are united by less.

—2393—

An exotic tribe penned by a quixotic scribe.

—2394—

Mountain of travails—valley of veils.

—2395—

The well knows how to dwell.

—2396—

The golden thread when woven is read.

—2397—

Re-tether a role to the central magnetic pole.

—2398—
Reign of quantity washed by a rain of quality.

—2399—
Presence is quintessence.

—2400—
Passive hero is an oxymoron.

—2401—
There is no well in hell.

—2402—
Boredom ravages inner kingdom.

—2403—
Introduce the world to induce itself.

—2404—
Truth can be refuted but not muted.

—2405—
Seasons are well-seasoned.

—2406—
Wear a muzzle to become a respected piece of the puzzle.

—2407—
To know a person read the face—
to know God stare at cosmic space.

—2408—

Earth of mirth under a ladder to the stars for rebirth.

—2409—

Choose perception—actor or spectator.

—2410—

Heart of creation beats as its own nation.

—2411—

Body is both tomb and womb.

—2412—

Raise the crops to praise—not succumb to malaise.

—2413—

Ultimate venture—the future.

—2414—

Druid influences the flow of fluid.

—2415—

Where to draw the boundary line to map of mind's mine.

—2416—

Flower the will to power.

—2417—

Irrational to approach the heavenly through the rational.

—2418—
Difficult to dispel gospel.

—2419—
Light can handle its candle.

—2420—
Ace creates space.

—2421—
Rob creativity with the robot.

—2422—
Thrill of free will.

—2423—
We are all relatives—absolutely.

—2424—
Sea gets high on weed.

—2425—
Language is its own gauge.

—2426—
Use the saw to see law and flaw.

—2427—
A vice will clamp down on anything nice.

—2428—

A queen bee has the sweet power to be.

—2429—

Moth does not weave cloth.

—2430—

Grammar was sentenced to being language hammer.

—2431—

Unbound reason is sound.

—2432—

God is beautician—not mathematician.

—2433—

Living as a hermit, life moves sideways.

—2434—

Awake at stake—a number will never slumber.

—2435—

Shaman God is pagan.

—2436—

True vision is not ever greater precision.

—2437—

Matter is immaterial.

—2438—
Made to repair or ode to despair.

—2439—
Humans whirling mirror the stars swirling—
Stars whirling mirror humans swirling.

—2440—
The philosopher's stone once begotten has been forgotten.

—2441—
By no stretch of the imagination is scholastic elastic.

—2442—
Devotion is the solution.

—2443—
Restore original beauty to even the score.

—2444—
A jade blade is never jaded.

—2445—
Enjoy is the most valuable toy.

—2446—
Face the face.

—2447—
Leaf is tree's sheath.

—2448—

Dogma is for dogs.

—2449—

Magic bounding line is never tragic.

—2450—

Vital sap is not its cap.

—2451—

Soul compass draws a circle around its oneness.

—2452—

Follow the nose to express and expose the prose pose.

—2453—

Escape—landscape mirrors mind-scape with the magical cape.

—2454—

Space age—more inner place than outer face or
more outer place than inner face.

—2455—

Jollity of Jupiter—not saturnine depression.

—2456—

Search for tranquility in the length and strength of agility.

—2457—

Synchronicity is the threshold to mystical city.

—2458—

God, as actor, searches for a star factor.

—2459—

Imagination is proclamation.

—2460—

Based on protein—we are naturally protean.

—2461—

The pilgrim lost in the world is grim.

—2462—

We are tall "sky-shapers."

—2463—

Psychology of the muse is music affecting psyche.

—2464—

Mind mirrors the universe by reflecting it.

—2465—

Feeling is healing.

—2466—

To conjugate personal verb takes the right mate.

—2467—

In the Truth car—style is a star.

—2468—

The truly religious are serious, not religious.

—2469—

The world is arcane mystery not mundane misery.

—2470—

Victim of the rhythm of dictum.

—2471—

The world will not sunder from the sound of thunder.

—2472—

Search for giant shoulders to perch.

—2473—

Strove towards the Ark treasured trove.

—2474—

Stars, plants and imagination fed by light.

—2475—

Coax a literary hoax.

—2476—

Animism is antidote to pessimism.

—2477—

Inner landscape dons its own natural escape cape.

—2478—

Ineffable is affable.

—2479—

Eidetic imagery can be prophetic sorcery.

—2480—

Balance bi-polar with equator.

—2481—

Trust ahead of yourself is not a bust.

—2482—

Bound to the book-of-nature we are covered.

—2483—

The tempest is a temperamental pest.

—2484—

Creativity burns to oppose the law of diminishing returns.

—2485—

Be hip to right the ship.

—2486—

The romantic is not monochromatic.

—2487—

Striving is reviving.

—2488—

Tracked down by picture of the future.

—2489—

Mired in longing to be admired.

—2490—

God does not know how not to dance.

—2491—

Better dance badly than walk boldly.

—2492—

Despair is lack of air.

—2493—

No purge for sexual urge.

—2494—

The game the Universe plays is its own name.

—2495—

The river does not know how not to flow.

—2496—

Lungs are full—air is heir.

—2497—

The 'Way of Tea' is a way to tee off harmony.

—2498—

Light can dream when a stream.

—2499—

Wisdom is something to cut the teeth on.

—2500—

Appetite is not lite.

—2501—

Not profanity, but pretending to be mad is proof of sanity.

—2502—

To be nothing is everything—to be everything is nothing.

—2503—

Predators prey—we actors pray.

—2504—

A photon is an angel turned on.

—2505—

Second wind is automatic rewind.

—2506—

Camouflaged in a herd of sheep, superman is still asleep

—2507—

Disrobe the habit of inferiority
to don globe of authority.

—2508—

Flower sexuality is cleverly stashed and unabashed.

—2509—

Spinoza had to grind lenses to find his senses.

—2510—

Prison infects—prism reflects.

—2511—

A sound wound heals itself.

—2512—

Poise oppose noise.

—2513—

Meet the ascetic and the aesthetic in the middle.

—2514—

A world in miniature completes the picture.

—2515—

Panpsychism heals the schism.

—2516—

Life is sound unbound.

—2517—

Become a scroll to allow visions to unroll.

—2518—

Great merchant can enchant.

—2519—

You hear what you are.

—2520—

The world stage is the sage.

—2521—

Lobotomy dictates dichotomy.

—2522—

The mean of meaning is not mean.

—2523—

Not know what you are doing but doing what you know.

—2524—

A solipsist has no desire to insist.

—2525—

An earthly ruler does measure everything.

—2526—

To not use the will is ill.

—2527—

Stirrup the paddle of the saddle.

—2528—

It does not follow we are innately hollow.

—2529—

Rex is the incarnation of codex.

—2530—

Try to step out of the tapestry of ancestry.

—2531—

Turn armor chinks to *amor links*.

—2532—

Ark is adventure park.

—2533—

In the flow outside of what we know.

—2534—

Worm view is the only form the bird knew.

—2535—

Escape the bullfighter's cape.

—2536—

Endure pain to counteract the natural bias of the brain.

—2537—

If you know what you are looking for you won't find it.

—2538—

A mental state hard fought is fraught with thought.

—2539—

Diffident—not different.

—2540—

Turn back on wild happiness for it to follow.

—2541—

Mars opened all its orange cape for fall to escape.

—2542—

Escape from the cave in a mystical nave.

—2543—

Epiphanic vision is not satanic.

—2544—

Enjoying what we have—we have what we enjoy.

—2545—

Dance penance—conquer the world with the pen.

—2546—

Conspire beyond desire.

—2547—

Skylark is half sky and half lark.

—2548—

One sees happiness turn to stone.

—2549—

Drenched in beauty—the reign of flowers entrenched.

—2550—

Light comes in a packet to wave as jacket.

—2551—

Life-raft is light.

—2552—

Lure—not trap, creating is more fishing than hunting with a map.

—2553—

Will the logician appear to the magician's spear to disappear.

—2554—

Cosmic face is space.

—2555—

Quicksilver prose is Mercury's rose.

—2556—

Mind dome is home.

—2557—

Sorcerer is source.

—2558—

Meaning is more means than ends.

—2559—

Life syllabus is not calculus nor counted with abacus.

—2560—

Lightning flash is enlightening splash.

—2561—

The Mind combo is mumbo jumbo.

—2562—

Can't treasure pure measure.

—2563—

Cannot track the soul taking a poll.

—2564—

Create one's own story is not illusory.

—2565—

Mage is true self-image.

—2566—

Understanding is one side of the brain eavesdropping on the other.

—2567—

No matter how hard fought—never seen a thought.

—2568—

Hypnogogic swath is the path.

—2569—

Thoth writing is Truth.

—2570—

Be content with right content.

—2571—

Enter the whole terrain through the rain.

—2572—

Nature of god is Nature.

—2573—

Pay the syntax.

—2574—

Soaring sublime plane or mired in profane.

—2575—

Air is heaven's stair.

—2576—

Vice to virtue—true sacrifice.

—2577—

Ouroboros cosmos beginnings are ends.

—2578—

Surprise is a natural guise to rise.

—2579—

Temper is temptation—

Patience is science—

Mind is contemplation.

—2580—

Know the cross of the crow.

—2581—

I am the eye—you are what you see.

—2582—

Happiness be guaranteed—or your life back.

—2583—

The book—both rook and nook.

—2584—

Individual in a duel is dual.

—2585—

Natural rhythm is no algorithm.

—2586—

Dance beauty—not permanence.

—2587—

Current is the river content.

—2588—

Forehead is foreknowledge.

—2589—

In the profound playground be both lost and found.

—2590—

Sheathe the sword in a rush—
breathe through calligrapher's brush.

—2591—

Sew to new—sow to know.

—2592—

In the labyrinth fight the Minotaur—
and in the ring the bull as centaur.

—2593—

No grime is a crime.

—2594—

The whole universe is not a black hole.

—2595—

Avoid ruts—create with guts.

—2596—

Numinous is not numerous.

—2597—
Repair the tear in the fabric—
a pair of pants or a universe that enchants.

—2598—
The tempest eye is at rest.

—2599—
True 'footnotes' are written with feet.

—2600—
Though out of mind—
the wunderkind can find mankind.

—2601—
Not blind—the invisible third eye completes the mind.

—2602—
Not blind-third eye completes the mind.

—2603—
Optics decides topics.

—2604—
God dances to create more chances.

—2605—
In the pool kingdom, the fool is wisdom.

—2606—
God is the ultimate "divining rod."

—2607—

Proving is not improving.

—2608—

Move to improve.

—2609—

Stationary writes you off.

—2610—

A real philosopher does not write philosophy.

—2611—

Be light to catch light.

—2612—

Strong is not wrong.

—2613—

Lower reason is treason.

—2614—

Light wave is not long but electrically strong.

—2615—

Idea is more real than reality.

—2616—

The Mind is smarter than you.

—2617—
It is unholy to pray to melancholy.

—2618—
No tuition for Intuition—
A science turns to nescience.

—2619—
Don't fail to trail the rail of the grail.

—2620—
Quicksand is no successful brand.

—2621—
Choose or lose.

—2622—
Intuition seeks uncertainty—
intellect reeks of certainty.

—2623—
Real Knowledge is an admixture of sense and nonsense.

—2624—
Protect the eye of the intellect.

—2625—
The tiniest sect is the insect.

—2626—
Whirl forms matter into a swirl.

—2627—

The world seen is sheen for the Unseen.

—2628—

Elevation is Revelation.

—2629—

Whirl will twirl matter into a spiral swirl.

—2630—

Proof is cleverly camouflaged spoof.

—2631—

An optician cannot help you see the right option.

—2632—

Seen from above,
a philosopher having fun
is tough love.

—2633—

God savors and favors bad dancers.

—2634—

Though an amateur is no auteur,
they are both in love with their tour.

—2635—

Enthusiasm is possessed by a god with a joyful nod.

—2636—
Evolution in thought is revolution fought.

—2637—
Ganesh, can't ignore—
the lucky elephant in the room
worth its weight in ore.

—2638—
Plow—leave fallow,
show—then follow.

—2639—
Inner leaks obscure vision of outer peaks.

—2640—
To expose the rose—prose rose to poetry.

—2641—
The passive fallacy is massive.

—2642—
Erotic is meteoric.

—2643—
Play with words to play with you.

—2644—
Nothing to do astonishing—hero is vanishing.

—2645—

Mind tower is its own power.

—2646—

A bridge to anywhere or no bridge to somewhere.

—2647—

Eternal fountain pushes the boulder up the mountain.

—2648—

In ancient curriculum encounter the summum bonum.

—2649—

A tree free of ornaments is free.

—2650—

Water seeks out original river ways—
the mind peaks in rays,

—2651—

The infatuated lover once smitten
becomes its own book to be written.

—2652—

Lie cannot stand itself.

—2653—

The game of fame is just a name.

—2654—

It's your pick—be well or be sick.

—2655—

A prose universe in poetic verse.

—2656—

All ladders start in the heart.

—2657—

Sing to the folly of melancholy.

—2658—

Words from a silver tongue
express the hands of a goldsmith.

—2659—

Energy fills up inside, in front, behind and to the side.

—2660—

Purpose of a plant is to grow a center,
purpose of a stone is to be center,
purpose of a man is to find center.

—2661—

Privilege has no edge on the ledge of knowledge.

—2662—

Imagination saves us from the fate of a low-energy state.

—2663—

The only time you know work is not play is when you count its day.

—2664—

Ordinary mind is a lie.

—2665—

Sky empty—moon full.

—2666—

Allow the target to follow the arrow.

—2667—

Faith and belief—two sides of the same leaf.

—2668—

You change things that change you.

—2669—

The head is a star,
the six senses are moons and planets
attracted from afar.

—2670—

The night beam is no daydream.

—2671—

Quality can never be proved.

—2672—

One percent that matters—
one degree of vitality reality.

—2673—
Complain softens the brain.

—2674—
Clueless—unable to recognize newness.

—2675—
Imagination is not about 'make believe' but 'believe-to-make.'

—2676—
Do—to know.

—2677—
Meaning can never be proved—only felt.

—2678—
Confidence in confidence is its own science.

—2679—
Plays are prayers and players are plays.

—2680—
Pull the rainbow—full of liquid arrow.

—2681—
Sow to reap takes the existential leap.

—2682—
Job did the job.

—2683—

Wide reading—glide spreading.

—2684—

The Pharaoh of the Ark's kingdom is Noah.

—2685—

The writer is writer—not righter.

—2686—

Life is no guided tour but tour de force connected to its source.

—2687—

Obscure is no cure for sure.

—2688—

Strive for the best—live through the rest.

—2689—

Creativity is meaningful activity.

—2690—

Write it to be true—to not be written off.

—2691—

Harvested wheat cannot be beat.

—2692—

Flower makes room to bloom.

—2693—

The miracle of transformation is the true nation.

—2694—

Notion of poetry is prose in motion.

—2695—

Can't tire of the world round—it's ground wire.

—2696—

Play safe in dry dock—
unable to take eyes off the clock.

—2697—

Presence of absence.

—2698—

Born humorously or reborn, as Nietzsche says—posthumously.

—2699—

Sane takes the higher plane.

—2700—

Overthink—push the Mind to the brink.

—2701—

Flow like the Nile—agile not fragile.

—2702—

Not drift—uplift.

—2703—

Amaze is not a maze.

—2704—

Fuse emotion with motion.

—2705—

A symbol is more real than reality.

—2706—

Romantic is never monochromatic.

—2707—

Need the left not left out—

for the right brain to get it right.

—2708—

Measure pleasure by its absence.

—2709—

Cult of beauty—not beauty of the cult.

—2710—

Roam interstellar space to find your race.

—2711—

Leap the modern—

reap ancient and future.

—2712—

Train with the heavy bag—
the body won't sag.

—2713—

Flying is trying.

—2714—

Empyrean favors protean.

—2715—

Sink a well—think well.

—2716—

Real beam is imaginary dream.

—2717—

Mystic outlet is magic carpet.

—2718—

Mental Nile is fertile.

—2719—

Know what's up—empty the cup.

—2720—

Artist face is gallery space.

—2721—

Light seed is original bulb.

—2722—

Sage can gauge age.

—2723—

Vision is both teacher and pupil mission.

—2724—

Numb to not succumb to what is dumb.

—2725—

Gold is bold and old—hot and cold.

—2726—

Consciousness for few is beauty anew.

—2727—

Not destined as planets—
suns bright light the night.

—2728—

Behold the cosmos unfold.

—2729—

Fire an arrow—follow its attire.

—2730—

Grow knowledge—sharpen its edge.

—2731—

Am I a tree imagining I am free—
or am I free thinking I am a tree?

—2732—

Individual is mutual.

—2733—

Sage travels with no baggage.

—2734—

Heal is the ultimate meal.

—2735—

Truth-less is ruthless.

—2736—

Rhyme makes time.

—2737—

Essay tries to say.

—2738—

Froth is the sea's cloth.

—2739—

God is pressure in the tire—

Man pumps to not tire.

—2740—

The mind has no designated room for gloom and doom.

—2741—

Beauty is the object of the subject and the subject of the object.

—2742—

A multitude can't buy gratitude.

—2743—

Handle with aplomb from birth to tomb.

—2744—

Adversity is diversity is university.

—2745—

A world before—created by metaphor.

—2746—

Battery recharged by driving—

the will by striving.

—2747—

Fires damped—muscles unused cramped.

—2748—

Curtain drawn hides dawn.

—2749—

Lucky blacksmith is also a cobbler

when forging a horseshoe.

—2750—

Track the whistle for what lies ahead not back.

—2751—

Outsider or insider—

beyond the box or boxed in.

—2752—

The brain is a horse to break, tame, saddle and train.

—2753—

Like the curve of the bell—

ring strong in the middle spell.

—2754—

Explore inner globe with frontal lobe.

—2755—

Between us and the All is a false wall.

—2756—

Too much happiness will kill the will.

—2757—

Search for meaning or

succumb to its demeaning.

—2758—

There is no comfort without discomfort.

—2759—

Hedonic treadmill breaks the will.

—2760—

It costs effort to pay the bill of free will.

—2761—

Vocation is vacation—vacation is not vocation.

—2762—

See is not free—there is an "action fee."

—2763—

Cranes fly in formation with a leader—
humans apply information without header.

—2764—

Bold drunk at the bar of gold.

—2765—

Art and Language—oracle and tabernacle.

—2766—

The body somatic is idiomatic.

—2767—

Words are food—feed the mood.

—2768—

A true sentence is for life.

—2769—

All is hidden until bidden.

—2770—

Each created petal strengthens its mettle.

—2771—

We are the problems we create.

—2772—

Think link—brain is chain.

—2773—

Clay tablet created the writing outlet day.

—2774—

Joke to break the yoke.

—2775—

Amps summon genies out of lamps.

—2776—

Transforming consciousness at will is a premier skill.

—2777—

Light as a feather at the end of the tether.

—2778—

A rose arose.

—2779—

Each task is its own mask and ask.

—2780—

Happy artist is no oxymoron.

—2781—

Cherish melancholia and love "La Folia."

—2782—

Not bad—just happy and sad.

—2783—

Age of consciousness as mirror is a mirage.

—2784—

The circle is the medicine man's oracle.

—2785—

Unhappiness is blinded by the sight of happiness.

—2786—

Understanding moves sideways.

—2787—

In the world of the 'confirmation bias,' stand alone on a dais.

—2788—

The seer saw the case to cut to the chase.

—2789—

Kill the chance—stop the dance.

—2790—
The dark age sees light at the end of a stark page.

—2791—
Follow one's own tail—
fail to find the trail.

—2792—
The tallest flower is closest to the rain shower.

—2793—
To know now is to plow—to plow now is to grow.

—2794—
We are the mistress of our own stress.

—2795—
The road is difficult to find—the find is the cult of the road.

—2796—
The dream is not in the pipe but its smoky steam.

—2797—
Recognize to disguise—the prize is the surprise.

—2798—
The original sentence was reticence.

—2799—
The ultimate objective is perspective.

—2800—

Drain the kingdom of magic—

boredom will reign tragic.

—2801—

Heaven of vitality opposes hell of triviality.

—2802—

The universe is wrought with thought.

—2803—

Both to field and wield—

God is gardener and shield.

—2804—

A bird's-eye view is beyond review.

—2805—

Intoxication is a voyage into the depths—

Vision is voyage into the heights.

—2806—

Altered states of consciousness are not united.

—2807—

Hierophant will chant—

elephant too large to enchant.

—2808—

Big Bang went out with a whimper—

never even sang.

—2809—

It takes measured precision to miss the vision.

—2810—

Every age is a cage to rewrite its page.

—2811—

Unfold the universe to behold its gold.

—2812—

Contentment is contagious.

—2813—

Build an imagination guild.

—2814—

Fire gets its attire from inspire.

—2815—

A clown's make-up is permanent—
an actor's permanence is to make-up.

—2816—

Which came first—the cosmos or its egg.

—2817—

Imagination nation—not stagnation.

—2818—

Dreaming meaning is not demeaning.

—2819—

Extra effort makes a holiday—not comfort.

—2820—

God's blot is a plot.

—2821—

Know the bow.

—2822—

No mystery in misery.

—2823—

On a lark there is no choice but to embark.

—2824—

Fewer words—longer explanation.

—2825—

World is meaning.

—2826—

Don't judge the wave before its nudge.

—2827—

Play joy like a toy.

—2828—

Muster what comes in a cluster.

—2829—
Mind is in the body—a body of work.

—2830—
A short life span aborts the master plan.

—2831—
The world as mine is a fine line.

—2832—
Strong to light long.

—2833—
A body of scripture fleshes out the picture.

—2834—
A philosopher-king knows what to bring.

—2835—
Pentagram sends its telegram.

—2836—
Man pleas, woman pleases.

—2837—
Power ideas shower and flower.

—2838—
Air of intrigue is its own league.

—2839—

An eccentric spins around its own center.

—2840—

Fly before walking—sing before talking.

—2841—

Purpose of despair is to repair its stair.

—2842—

It is not the crown that makes the queen but the sheen.

—2843—

Mind of God is God in Mind.

—2844—

Mind strayed is betrayed.

—2845—

Mouth speaks source of river course.

—2846—

See things as they are—
from the perspective of a star.

—2847—

Low esteem runs out of steam.

—2848—

Explain time listening to its chime.

—2849—
Beauty is intelligence—intelligence is beauty.

—2850—
Sumer lights the original summer.

—2851—
Architectonic is its own tonic.

—2852—
Hue of human is celestial blue.

—2853—
A fragment of a phrase is the fragrance.

—2854—
Begotten is not forgotten.

—2855—
Tall shoots from deep roots.

—2856—
Formal logic a straitjacket
to keep words within its bracket.

—2857—
Kaleidoscope sees more than microscope.

—2858—
Spinning in its stance—
Renaissance becomes the dance.

—2859—
Inside the mystical home is the sound of "om."

—2860—
Where the body ends—
the outline transcends.

—2861—
The first play was written in clay.

—2862—
No malice—the mind is a chalice.

—2863—
Happiness gets in the way of self-actualization.

—2864—
Rain outside—inside no pain.

—2865—
A dive for the pearl finds its necklace live.

—2866—
The plot is the knot.

—2867—
Whether in heaven or hell
God knows our number well.

—2868—
Glow in the perpetual now.

—2869—

In rhyme there is reason.

—2870—

In the engagement rings the wedding sings.

—2871—

The mystery of symmetry is asymmetry.

—2872—

Too old to be bold the spirit is sold.

—2873—

A prime number doesn't suffer from self-division.

—2874—

In a constant hurry life is blurry.

—2875—

Getting high on words should be illegal.

—2876—

Cuneiform used to be uniform

—2877—

Fire can play in a library with tablets of clay.

—2878—

The winged chariot cannot be driven by any idiot.

—2879—

Reveal to heal.

—2880—

Awake the snake.

—2881—

Ear is spatial—not linear.

—2882—

Spiritual sap rises to fill the gap.

—2883—

Grow inside—know outside,
know inside—grow outside.

—2884—

Eclectic is electric.

—2885—

Our own portmanteau: man-kind.

—2886—

Chains freed with brains.

—2887—

Codes of seeing transform unknown modes of being.

—2888—

A log chose its own spot to rot.

—2889—

A camp of concentration is not a concentration camp.

—2890—

Pineal is real.

—2891—

Because the mind can be lost it was once yours.

—2892—

The main purpose of the brain is to halt an energy drain.

—2893—

Be the Way or in the way—

that is the question

—2894—

Beatitude is beauty plus attitude.

—2895—

Be cheerful—not fearful or tearful.

—2896—

To know is to not know.

—2897—

Fire is the ground wire.

—2898—

God speaks openly in symbols.

—2899—

Circumscribe—not square the scribe.

—2900—

First—dial primordial.

—2901—

Man is the system—not part of one.

—2902—

Infinite eight supports its own weight

—2903—

Difficult to turn the table on comfortable.

—2904—

Fill the quill, electrify the will.

—2905—

Diffidence and indifference don't make a difference.

—2906—

Knowledge is beauty—beauty is knowledge.

—2907—

Succeed contains both its own need and seed.

—2908—

Modern science is rarely scientific.

—2909—

Fulfilling is not filling.

—2910—

Stand alone to set the tone.

—2911—

Wax and wane, candlelight melts its cane.

—2912—

Adult is a secret vault.

—2913—

No praise for malaise.

—2914—

Erection is resurrection.

—2915—

Review the toy—renew the joy.

—2916—

When noticed—happiness is sadness.

—2917—

Plight interconnects flight to light.

—2918—

Vitalism overcame dualism.

—2919—

Shaman, not shame, is the true man's name.

—2920—

Ordinary gravity—extraordinary levity.

—2921—

Winning is planet spinning.

—2922—

Heaven and hell remarried at the source of their divorce.

—2923—

Paradise had to be lost to be found.

—2924—

The indifferent threshold is stone cold.

—2925—

We have everything and nothing.

—2926—

Flair is its own air.

—2927—

How, not why—is now.

—2928—

The most tantalizing allure—
security is never secure.

—2929—
Welder is true elder.

—2930—
Older but not bolder.

—2931—
Universal log is dialog.

—2932—
Ideas of formation are beyond information.

—2933—
Mind light—faster than the speed of sight.

—2934—
Earth is not flat but rounded sharp.

—2935—
True logic is not logical.

—2936—
What you've laughed cannot be stolen.

—2937—
An atlas of bliss outlines key territories not to miss.

—2938—
Self-belief is a powerful chief.

—2939—

Global mirth narrowed its girth since mythical birth.

—2940—

Ambition and sloth are not cut from the same cloth.

—2941—

The true hunter is own prey—to spir-it.

—2942—

Will is magic potion in motion.

—2943—

Discovery is recovery.

—2944—

Circumstance yields to dance.

—2945—

Smaller the bird—bigger the song.

—2946—

Mischief is part of being chief.

—2947—

Right type needs no hype.

—2948—

No detox from paradox.

—2949—

Explain light in waves or particles—

fail to see the "light brain."

—2950—

Sphere of Mind revolves around Here.

—2951—

Leisure is work—work is pleasure.

—2952—

Forms inside are outside—forms outside are inside.

—2953—

Naturally stoic, plants are heroic.

—2954—

A traditional bard is in charge of the yard.

—2955—

Galaxy shaped like a spiral horn,

planet earth is a grain of corn.

—2956—

Work is there to both find and lose yourself.

—2957—

Magnet is present net.

—2958—

True beauty is both alien and familiar.

—2959—
The amoeba foot is false to boot.

—2960—
Imagination sought is already taught.

—2961—
Grab is not to grasp.

—2962—
True vacation is education—true education is vacation.

—2963—
Ripples are wave nipples.

—2964—
Air, water, land and fire—philosopher's first attire

—2965—
Live "inner car" will strive to drive.

—2966—
Find outer through inner.

—2967—
Ancient dig is a dream gig.

—2968—
Exalt or come to a halt.

—2969—

Wave rolls to save.

—2970—

Philosophy—psychedelic as ancient relic.

—2971—

Evolutionary pond lies beyond.

—2972—

Strength is more intelligent than Intelligence.

—2973—

Own Inner sources—the only show in town.

—2974—

Left brain muddle—the right will huddle.

—2975—

Eclectic present is electric present.

—2976—

The universe is a rhyme of itself—in prose and verse.

—2977—

Blundering cloud can hover over thundering lover.

—2978—

Particles of spiritual light
in a prison of material might.

—2979—

Pleroma emanates light aroma.

—2980—

Pinning down "reality" will never reveal its spinning totality.

—2981—

To peak means no leak.

—2982—

Labor to harbor—shoe to canoe.

—2983—

Reams of books or dreams of brooks.

—2984—

Roam home to Rome.

—2985—

Bold to amplify the Mind one hundredfold.

—2986—

Madness is the health of the future.

—2987—

Vision sees the world with no division.

—2988—

Disappear to be found—

hear to resound.

—2989—

Flow of the stream is seam of the dream.

—2990—

Fire guides—the world hides.

—2991—

Fun is its own explosive gun.

—2992—

City way of many is mediocrity.

—2993—

Force imagination—source of creation.

—2994—

The philosopher's pallet is an efficient cleanser.

—2995—

Create a giant or be a worker ant.

—2996—

Find a god wherever you trod.

—2997—

The sheep astray lit the day.

—2998—

Withstand the rains of high terrains.

—2999—

Life came forth from the froth of Thoth.

—3000—

Higher glyphs are hieroglyphs.

ABOUT THE AUTHOR

David L. Laing is a visionary self-taught artist and writer currently living and working in Seattle, Washington. His works in oil, acrylic, watercolor, and pen and ink drawing have been exhibited in South America, the United States, and Europe.

David expatriated in his early twenties and headed for South America with no money, in hopes of finding or founding a "New Paris for artists." Two months later and thirty pounds lighter, he limped into São Paulo, Brazil, having traversed the entire continent overland, nearly ten thousand miles, surviving purely on his own wits and with the aid of a few helpful souls. David spent over fifteen years in Brazil writing, painting, and composing music.

Since his return to the USA, David has focused on book publishing of his own novels, art books, and compilations of his articles. Solar Codex: A Light Odyssey and Notes from the Milky Way are the first two volumes in the quartet of Cosmic Adventure novels. At present, he is working on the other two novels to complete the quartet and is preparing for publication many new books of drawings, articles, dialogs, plays, and screenplays. Most of David's written work is lavishly illustrated with literally hundreds of drawings, all hand-inked by him.

PURCHASING ARTWORK AND CONNECTING WITH DAVID L. LAING

ARTWORK

Drawings and paintings from David L. Laing's books and other themed collections may be purchased at his Cosmic Art Center page on ArtPal, www.artpal.com/davidllaing. His work is available as fine art prints, canvas prints, custom framed prints, and even mugs.

WEBSITE AND EMAIL LIST

- Website: Find David's books, artwork and more at www.davidllaing.com
- Email newsletter: Subscribe at davidllaing.com for news about book releases, art collections, exhibits, and more.
- Instagram: Follow David at instagram.com/davidl.laing
- Twitter: Follow David at twitter.com/davidllaing9
- YouTube: See book trailers and animated illustrations at https://www.youtube.com/@davidllaing

ARTSANA VIDEO AND YOUTUBE CHANNEL

Watch the video of David's art book, *Artsana, 35 Sacred Yoga Asanas Expressed Through Art*, at tinyurl.com/artsana-video. Produced by One Field Media, www.onefieldmedia.com, and David L. Laing, this short film features eight extra-ordinary yogis, accompanied with music by Andre Feriante, www.andreferiante.com.

ALSO BY DAVID L. LAING

ART AND COLORING BOOKS

Higher Glyphs

Artsana: 35 Sacred Yoga Asanas Expressed Through Art

Alpha 2 Zulu: Military Alphabet Coloring Book

AlphaBetter: Coloring Book of Letters and Numbers

Ancient Runes: For Coloring and Meditation

Kolor Khmer: A Creative Cambodian Alphabet Coloring Book

Willing Evolution

Dance of the Dance

ANTHOLOGIES

ARTICLES

Beyond the Box, Volume 1

Beyond the Box, Volume 2

Beyond the Box, Volume 3 [Forthcoming]

Beyond the Box, Volume 4 [Forthcoming]

APHORISMS

Not Yet Human

Almost Human

Just Human

Fully Human

Beyond Human [Forthcoming]

COSMIC ADVENTURE QUARTET - NOVELS

Solar Codex: A Light Odyssey

Notes from the Milky Way

Pentagram Rising [Forthcoming]

Prometheus Reforged [Forthcoming]

PLATONIC DIALOGUE STYLE BOOKS

Minds Beyond Time: A Cosmic Colloquium

Thinking and Drinking: A Cocktail Party of the Minds

Presidents in Paradise [Forthcoming]

www.ingramcontent.com/pod-product-compliance
Lightning Source LLC
Chambersburg PA
CBHW032149040426
42449CB00005B/458